D1515199

CRAYON TALKS

CRAYON TALKS

By

L. O. BROWN
Author of "Chalk Talks," etc.

NEW YORK
Fleming H. Revell Company
LONDON AND EDINBURGH

Printed in the United States of America

New York: 158 Fifth Avenue
London: 21 Paternoster Square

FOREWORD

THAT the eye-gate has a far greater appeal than the ear-gate is a fact generally accepted—a picture having been said to be "worth a thousand words."

One need not be an artist to take advantage of the eye-gate method here set forth, for the simplified drawings in this book make it possible for anyone to illustrate these talks before an audience with a few easily drawn strokes.

The public speaker, lecturer, teacher, missionary, evangelist, preacher and minister who presents facts in pictures pleasingly conveys truth through the most impressive, attractive and lasting method.

The author in his years of experience has found the using of the crayon, while speaking to an audience, a most entertaining and helpful way of attracting and holding the interest of both "grown-ups" and children.

It is the author's cherished thought that, once the reader uses this plan, he will be inspired to make crayon presentation a part of his regular program for the future.

L. O. Brown

Indianapolis, Ind.

CONTENTS

1

MY FIRST LESSON

"I am come that they might have life, and that they might have it more abundantly."—JOHN 10:10.

PERHAPS you are not aware of the fact that I at one time took some lessons in drawing.

Let me tell you about it. I made a drawing of two trees. They were oaks as near as I can remember. After satisfying myself that it was as good as I could do, I took it to my teacher.

She said, "That is fine, but it lacks something." I wondered what it lacked. She said, "Your picture lacks atmosphere, distance, toning value, foreground, and a centerpiece." I began to think it lacked the whole thing. She said, as she began to work on the picture, "If you put a little purple in the sky, that will give atmosphere. Should you put an old fence in here, coming over the hill, that will give distance. Another fence will lend more distance. Toning value will help the trees and foliage. An old roadway would make the foreground. Then the centerpiece." I wondered where she would put it, when she said, "Let's put in the picture as the centerpiece an old buggy going over the hill. This will do nicely. Now the picture has a reason for being."

Years have passed, and as I think back over the many changes that have come we can well use the picture to represent life.

So many things we are in need of in this life, it almost staggers us to think of all of them. But by taking one thing at a time, following the suggestion of the great Teacher, we will get toning value, distance, atmosphere, and a grand foreground, with the center thought that of Christ.

2

DEVELOPMENT

"The entrance of thy word giveth light."—PSALM 119:130.

MANY years have passed since the beginning of this country. The labor, privation, and suffering which have been necessary for our forefathers to endure in order to make this country what it is, can never be fully realized by the present and coming generations. Many changes have taken place and perhaps many more will follow.

When the sturdy Norsemen came to this country they found great forests of virgin timber. These forests gave, and as they disappeared the fertile fields began to show. The soil gave, and the coal mines were the result. The coal gave, and coke was produced. The coke gave, and the iron became an asset. Iron gave, and oil was found. Oil gave, and gas was produced. Gas gave, and heat and light were the result. Light gave, and electricity came. Electricity gave, and power was harnessed. Power gave, and the means of travel are made easy. All of these valuable assets have become ours because of sacrifice and development.

The forests, the soil, the coal, the coke, the iron, the oil, the gas, the light, the electricity, all have given, and out of these sacrifices we are enjoying a different age in the old world, the same old world.

The work of the church has developed down through the ages because of the different consecrated men who gave their lives in promotion of the kingdom of God.

Many new methods have been adopted in the development of the church, but the plan of redemption remains the same. The old gospel never changes.

PREPARING THE LESSON

"Study to show thyself approved unto God, a workman that needeth not to be ashamed, rightly dividing the word of truth."—II TIMOTHY 2:15.

TO TEACH the Sunday-school lesson correctly should be the desire of every teacher, and a lesson to be taught must first be studied that the teacher may know that he knows. Then the teacher should present the truth in such an interesting way that it will not be forgotten. Almost any one can go before a class and talk, filling up the time, perhaps, with an interesting story. But teaching is more than this.

Any one can make lines on a sheet of paper, but it takes more than lines to make a picture. It requires that the lines be placed in certain directions so that the desired object may be reproduced . . . let me illustrate ——————— These lines are not a picture, and any one could place them on the paper just so ——————— But to make a rose it will be necessary to make a stem with its stickers, and to round out the petals with shadows and high lights. Then a bud bending over ready to bloom would add balance to the picture.

In teaching the Sunday-school lesson, one should handle it as the rose is produced. One should come from a review of last Sunday's lesson into the full grown truth of the lesson to be taught, and reach over into the next Sunday's lesson, previewing it in such a way that it will create interest, so that each member of the class will want to be present next Sunday and see it bloom. Those who always spend their time looking back are like the stem only. Those who spend all their time with the present problems of life without a review of the past, are like the rose without a stem—no foundation. Those who spend their time looking forward, dreaming of the future, are like the bud only. No one of these parts alone is ideal. It takes the well-rounded stem, the full-blown rose, and the growing bud to make the ideal picture or lesson.

4

CONTRARY WINDS

"For the winds were contrary."—MATTHEW 14:24.

A GENTLEMAN was watching the planes at a large airport as they were landing and taking off. A pilot standing near him said, "How would you like to go up for a ride?" "Oh," he said, "I would enjoy it very much indeed." The pilot said, "I am going up in a few minutes and will take you along; just come with me to the hangar." The plane was run out and made ready for the flight. The men climbed in and taxied out to the farthest edge of the field. There the pilot turned the plane around and was ready for the take-off.

The man touched the pilot on the shoulder and asked, "Why did you come out here?" The pilot replied, "We must take off against the wind, as it gives greater speed in less time and shorter distance, and helps to lift the plane into the air." With this explanation, they started. A quick climb lifted them above the trees, lakes, and city, where the plane could be turned in any direction and not be affected to any great extent by the winds.

Many times the problems of life come blowing hard against us—the tests, the trials, the crosses, the disappointments and the sorrows. It is then we need that upward pull of faith which comes by facing these contrary winds and using them to lift us above the things that annoy, and so put us in a position where we can make progress in the Christian life.

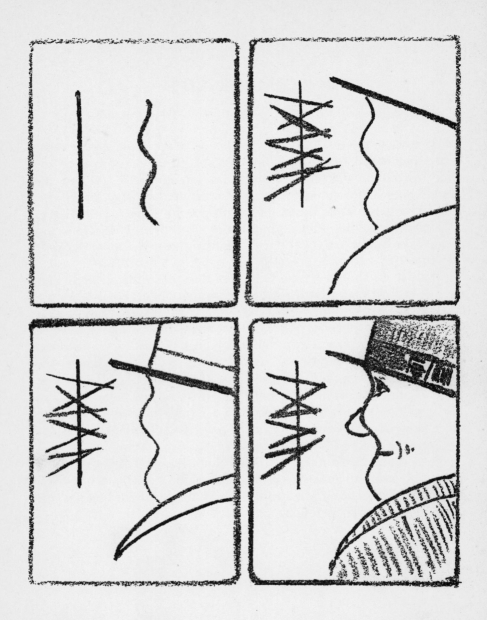

THE STRAIGHT LIFE

"Prove all things; hold fast that which is good."—I THESSALONIANS 5:21.

IT IS always interesting to any audience to see some one or more persons called to the front to perform. Have some boy or girl come up on the platform and make a straight line. (When the straight line is drawn, ask him to draw a crooked line. After this is done, call for some other person to do the same. Tell him to make a straight line, then to make a crooked line. If the lines are parallel, a lesson may be drawn showing we are unconsciously influenced by others.)

Now, if we should try to tack cross lines onto the straight line, we would find that it still remains a straight line. So it is with a straight life. If one tacks on to a straight life, it does not change the life nor the purpose of it. The crooked line is like a crooked life. The minute you begin tacking on to a crooked life, just that soon it begins to change and is not at all what the original life was intended to be, and it is not long until it is being laughed at.

The one who would not be laughed at should keep straight. There will be no chance to tack onto a straight life anything that can change it, for through all of life's tests and trials there is the one purpose, that of keeping straight.

It seems easier to make a crooked line than a straight one, and also it is easier to make a crooked life than a straight one. For the crooked life has no restraint, while the straight life has the teachings of Jesus to follow.

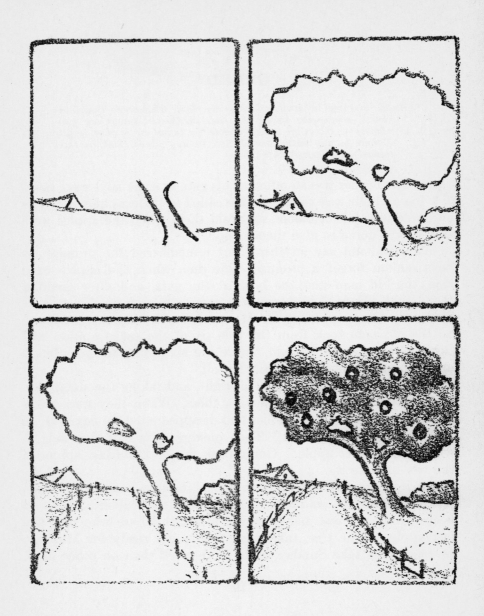

6

GREED

"Finally, brethren, whatsoever things are true, whatsoever things are honest, whatsoever things are just, whatsoever things are pure, whatsoever things are lovely, whatsoever things are of good report; if there be any virtue, and if there be any praise, think on these things."—PHILIPPIANS 4:8.

AN OLD farmer was standing at his gate as some boys were passing on their way to school. He called to them as he pointed to an apple tree full of bloom, and told them when the apples were ripe he was going to give them some.

They did not say anything, but remembered the promise, as boys seldom forget a promise. One day, when the apples were ripe, the old man met the boys at the gate, and after greeting them, said, "Boys, I promised you some apples from this tree. I have only seven apples on it. However, I will keep my promise." So the old man took from the tree six of the seven apples, and turning to the boys, he said, "Here are six apples for you, but I am keeping one on the tree for myself."

The boys thought that was all right, and taking the six apples, they started down the road, eating them. When they were nearing home, the last of the apples had disappeared. One boy said, "I wish I had another apple." Then picking up a club, he said, "I will have another apple." Going back, he beat the last apple off the tree and ate it.

God has given us six days in which to labor, visit, and be entertained, and He wants us to remember the Sabbath day and keep it holy, for rest and worship. Many there are who beat the last apple off the tree, taking Sunday to get ready for Monday. In fact, some take Sunday to do more work than on other days.

THE OPOSSUM HUNT

"Go forward."—Exodus 14:15.

ONE fine evening a man decided to go opossum hunting. Securing a sack and lantern, he started out. He was not out long before he came to a small tree with an opossum in it. He shook the tree and down came Mr. Opossum. When he hit the ground and rolled over as if he were dead, the hunter took the opossum by the tail and dropped him in his sack. Looking around at the other bushes to see if there were other opossums, he saw one running along on the ground. So he grabbed it by the tail and slipped it in the sack. He said to himself, "Now I have two, and that is not so bad."

Hearing a sound behind him, he turned again, and there was a third opossum close to the sack. Grabbing it by the tail, he turned to his sack, and on investigating, found that all he had was a hole in the corner of the sack. The opossum he held by the tail was the one he had been catching all evening.

Quite often efforts are put forth in our churches and Sunday schools, or organizations, but the work has to be done over and over again because of the leaks. Many times the leaks are letting valuable people drop, with no way of bringing them back.

It should be the business of the superintendent and teachers to help the pastor to plan to stop the leak by more efficient work.

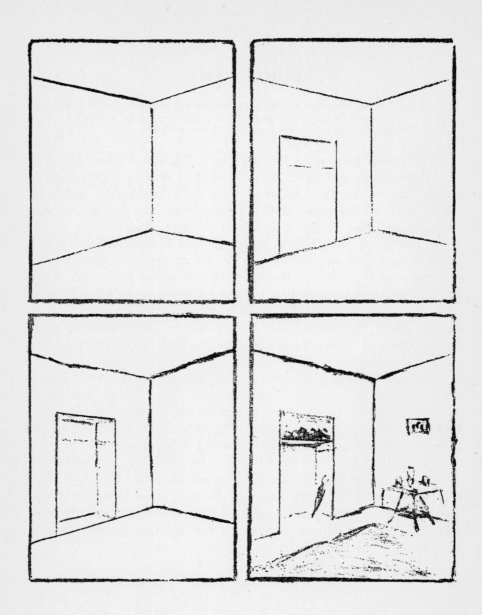

PRICE PAID

"I beseech you therefore, brethren, by the mercies of God, that ye present your bodies a living sacrifice, holy, acceptable unto God, which is your reasonable service."—ROMANS 12:1.

TWO young men were looking for a furnished room to rent. After looking one over, they decided to take it, supposing, of course, that when they returned with their trunks the landlady would have all her personal belongings removed. But not so, for the room was just as they had seen it the first time.

In the closet stood a large umbrella, and as they had umbrellas of their own they would have no use for it. So they placed it in the center of the room on the floor. On the closet shelf were some ladies' hats, but as they had no use for them, they placed them with the umbrella. On the walls hung portraits of people they did not know, and feeling that they would be better satisfied with the portraits of their own friends, they added the pictures to the pile on the floor.

The next morning the young men left for their work. When they returned at noon, the landlady said, "Now, boys, I want to apologize for leaving all these things in the room. You did right to place them on the floor, and if there is anything else you do not care for, just put it on the floor and I will remove it."

The Master has paid the price for our salvation, and when He enters our heart life, the umbrella of selfish pride that has been used to ward off the truth must go. He may show us other things which might interfere with our growth in the Christian life that will also have to be removed before He can take possession and fully occupy our hearts.

NO TRESPASSING

"The wisdom of the prudent is to understand his way."—Proverbs 14:8.

TWO business men planned to go rabbit hunting. One of them had a friend, George Grey, who was a farmer. They asked him for the privilege of hunting on his farm, and it was granted.

The men started on their quest for game. They failed to ask concerning the boundary lines of the farm, and on they went, from one field to another, until late in the afternoon they came through a woods to the big highway, where they saw a sign on a tree which read, "NO TRESPASSING." It was printed in large letters, and underneath, in smaller letters, was the name of the owner of the farm, L. E. Jones.

The men were very much surprised to learn that they had spent most of the afternoon hunting on forbidden territory and had trespassed unintentionally.

There are those who wish to do the right thing in the service of the Master and would not intentionally violate any known law of God. However, sometimes these are the ones who, for lack of knowledge of the territory they are in, trespass on the territory of youth with killing effect.

At the close of a musical program, a boy came up to the man who had played the cornet and said, "My father is going to get me a cornet when I learn to play the piano." The man said, "Oh, don't learn to play the piano. That is only for sissies, don't bother with it, just learn to play the cornet." This man was trespassing in territory he did not know, for after this remark the father and mother could not get their son to continue his lessons on the piano. He learned to play the cornet, but years later he said, "Dad, I wish now I had learned to play the piano."

10

DECEPTION

"For if a man think himself to be something, when he is nothing, he deceiveth himself."—GALATIANS 6:3.

IF I should spend the time that is allotted to me for this crayon lesson, just drawing straight lines and making marks, it would, of course, be a crayon talk, and I would be getting by with my agreement, but you would be disappointed I fear.

Should these lines be finished into something with handles on it, you would begin to draw on your imagination and try to solve the mystery of what it is intended to be. You might take it to be a saw, or, with its two handles, it might resemble a fruit dish. Then, again, it could possibly represent an accordion, or even a casket.

A saw is quite valuable if you have some one who is willing to use it. A fruit dish is good if it is filled with delicious fruit. An accordion makes fine music if one is efficient in his art, but if not, it makes a dreadful discord. A casket is used to lay away the dead. There are many people who are dead and do not know it. They are just walking around saving funeral expenses. They are dead in a different sense, of course—dead to the greater things of life.

However, this picture, when finished, shows us that part of the truth was not the whole truth, for deception can enter into a very small place. The whole truth is always best, for there are times that if the whole truth were known, one's back would be turned, revealing that it is not at all what it was supposed to be.

There are many deceptions in life, and things are not always what they seem. We should not jump at conclusions until the whole truth is brought before us.

We are easily deceived by a magician or a sleight-of-hand performer, but the enemy of our soul is even more subtle, because he makes a part of the truth seem like the whole truth.

THE RIVER

"It was not disobedient unto the heavenly vision."—ACTS 26:29.

IT WAS a fine summer day, the air was balmy, and the atmosphere was scented with the fragrance of the fields. A country visitor made his way over a road he had traversed many times before, at all times of the day and night. This time he was surprised, as he looked ahead of him, to see a man sitting by the roadside in a chair. As he came nearer, he discovered the man was an artist painting a picture of the scenery near by.

The artist had selected his motive and was placing his mass of colors in so well that it was easy to imagine what the picture would be like before it was finished. "Oh," said the visitor to the artist, "you have left the river out of the picture." The artist replied, "Watch me awhile and you will see I have not forgotten. I am just getting ready with the right kind of surroundings to put the river in its place." With a few short strokes, a touch here and a touch there, the river was in the center of the picture, a beautiful flowing stream of water.

Many times there are those of us who fail to leave room in our life's picture for the things worth while. Our view is so foreshortened by conditions and circumstances that the center or heart life is overlooked and the life giving stream is omitted, until the great Artist with His hand of love reaches down and with His touch of love, here and there, puts into our lives the thing that is vital, the stream of love that flows out to all mankind, making life of true value.

12

OPPOSITION

"And we know that all things work together for good to them that love God."—ROMANS 8:28.

A STORY is told of a young blacksmith who met and fell in love with the daughter of an artist. They spent happy hours together. Finally the young man got up courage enough to call on the father.

As the young blacksmith stepped into the studio, the artist looked up from his painting and said, "Well, what are you wanting?" "Sir," said the young man, "I came to ask you for your daughter, I love her and want her to become my wife." The artist replied, "Young man, I have no fault to find in you, but I can not have my daughter marry a man with as low a position as a mere blacksmith." This was a great disappointment to the young man and it was hard for him to meet this opposition. He could not give up his trade, neither was he willing to give up the girl. So he decided he would elevate his position, and he began studying metal craft and ironwork, making different artistic designs.

After months of study and labor, he became an artist in metal work, making a name for himself greater even than that of the father of the girl.

The opposition was overcome, the father was glad to give his consent to the marriage of his daughter to the metal-craft artist.

There are disappointments in life which may seem hard to bear, and yet they may be made stepping-stones to a far better way if the right spirit is used and the opposition is overcome.

AFRAID TO VENTURE

"For it is God which worketh in you both to will and to do of his good pleasure."—PHILIPPIANS 2:13.

A MISSIONARY in the southern part of Ohio visited, by invitation, a small rural Sunday school to give an address on Sunday-school work.

He was greeted at the door by the superintendent and was told that they would appreciate any suggestion he wished to offer. "Just put them all in our Sunday-school wagon and we will move it along," said the superintendent.

In his address, the missionary said that every Sunday school should be well organized, with cradle roll, home department, teacher training, organized classes, missionary society, etc. He said that the superintendent should not try to do things alone, but should use his teachers and officers to help him carry out these valuable suggestions, which were sure to bring new life into the school.

Six months later, the missionary chanced to visit that same Sunday school again, and as the same superintendent met him at the door, he asked, "Well, how is your school progressing by this time? Did you try out any of the suggestions I left with you?" "Well," said the superintendent, "everything is about the same as when you were here. Your suggestions were fine, but we just seemed to be afraid to try anything new, so we are still in the same old rut."

They had left all the suggestions left with them piled up on their "Sunday-school wagon," as the superintendent called it, and had run it out under the tree of indifference which grows close to every Sunday school, and left it there. This tree thrives on unconcern and has the fruit of do-nothing on it. The shadow of this tree is sure to fall across any new suggestion that comes along unless the superintendent keeps the Sunday-school wagon moving along in the glorious sunshine of opportunity and service.

THE SHIP ON THE SAND BAR

"For we are labourers together with God."—I CORINTHIANS 3:9.

A GREAT concourse of people had gathered. They were waiting for the moment to arrive when the new ship, with its great white sails, should be loosed from its moorings to float out into the ocean on its maiden trip.

When the appointed time came, the ship was loosed from its moorings and passed out into a glassy sea, amid a chorus of cheers and the waving of handkerchiefs.

Days, weeks, and months passed into years. The ship faced many a gale and stood the test of many a storm.

One day the old captain saw a storm rising and the overhanging clouds growing black. He turned to the pilot and asked him what he thought they had best do. The pilot knew the ship was old and could not stand many more storms, so he advised that they try to reach home as soon as possible.

The billows began dashing high, tossing the ship to and fro. It was a long way around into the harbor, so they turned the ship toward home, a short way across.

The ship had scarcely gone twice its length when it plowed deeply into a sand bar, which held it fast. The sails were being torn by the raging storm in sight of home.

A message was signaled across, and loved ones ran out the old cannon and shot a line to the ship. It was made fast to the ship. Then every man on the shore was asked to pull, but the ship would not come loose. Then the rope was lengthened and the women took hold and pulled but it did not come loose. The children were asked to help, and the men, women, and children, all took hold of the rope and they all pulled together and the ship came loose.

Out in the billows of sin are loved ones who need our united effort in order to bring them home to Jesus.

WILD TURKEYS

"Surely he shall deliver thee from the snare of the fowler, and from the noisome pestilence."—PSALM 91:3.

BACK in the pioneer days there were many wild turkeys.

In the fall of the year, when the farmers wanted wild turkeys, they would haul rails out into an open space and build a pen with rails across the top. Then they would dig a trench, with one end leading into the pen, the other outside. This trench was deep enough for a turkey to pass under the bottom rail of the pen with his head down. Outside the pen the trench would reach about fifteen feet. They were then ready for the shelled corn, for every trap must have its bait. They put some of the corn in the trench on the inside and scattered the rest on the outside.

Soon the turkeys would come flying over, and, seeing something new, they would fly down and rest on the pen. Then their attention would be attracted to the corn. They would begin to eat it, picking it up a grain at a time until they had followed along up to the pen, and they would keep right on eating, with their heads down, until they were inside and were trapped.

The Prodigal Son was lured away by sin until he was very far from his father's house. One day, when money and friends were gone and there was no food or clothing, he realized he was trapped. The devil can make sin alluring and tempt you with the pleasures of the world, and make you think you are all right until you realize the bait is gone and you are trapped and left alone. Only God can make a way of escape, which is through repentance and returning to Him, through His Son Jesus Christ, our Saviour and Redeemer.

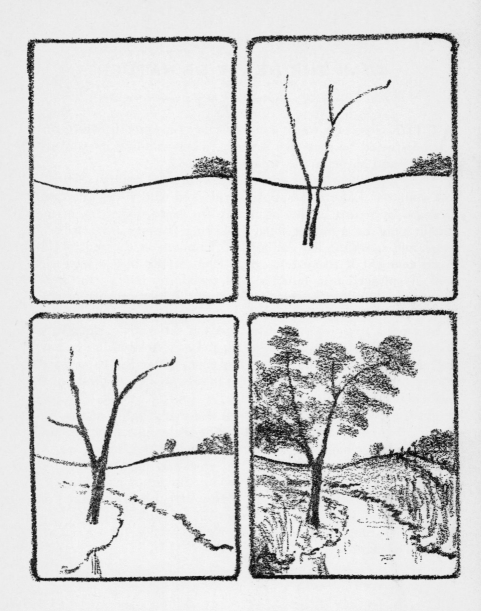

NEAR THE HEART OF NATURE

"Great is the Lord, and greatly to be praised."—PSALM 48:1.

AT THE close of a warm summer's day the smooth, white turn-pike could be seen like a great ribbon winding its way over the hills and through the valley.

Here and there overhanging trees of rare beauty cast their soft shadows. Elderberries, pokeberries, and wild vines, artistically arranged by nature, added beauty to the scene. Near by, a small stream sang its gurgling song, frolicking happily from ledge to ledge, and sparkling like millions of diamonds in the sunset glow. For a moment it seemed to rest. Then diving into a mirrorlike pool, it splashed into bubbles, and remaining but an instant, it danced on its merry course to the river. While pausing to get a better view of the surroundings, our attention is called by the croaking of a frog to a tuft of tall grass at the water's edge. In the distance the hoot of an owl is heard, and as if answering, the katydid responds with its long piercing zing. Then the chirp of the cricket asks another question, but is interrupted by the buzz of the jarfly and the trill of the tree toad.

As the evening shadows deepen, the many lights of the little fireflies twinkle and are reflected in the water like so many stars, while the beetle band, with its evening melody resounding o'er hill and dale, brings forth this hooting, croaking, buzzing, humming, piping, trilling, chirping, hissing, cooing, discord of melody.

God has planned it all for us. Every little blade of grass, every little bug and insect, takes pleasure in its task of praise to its Maker. We, too, should praise Him for His wonderful works to the children of man.

TIME

"Redeeming the time."—Colossians 4:5.

HOW often we waste the precious moments which are ours, forgetting that time never returns, that it can neither be stored nor postponed, but flies on at a never changing speed.

The watch which is used for keeping the time often runs too fast or too slow and sometimes needs to be adjusted in order to be accurate.

The chief qualification of a good watch is accuracy. Trains must be run on schedule time to avert wrecks and give the public prompt service, which is greatly appreciated, although many times no word of commendation is given.

An engineer had brought his train to a stop at the station; and as he swung down out of the cabin, with his oil can in hand, to give the engine a good greasing, a group of four traveling men stopped and one of them said, "Sir, we have taken up a gift among the traveling men on this train to show our appreciation of your getting us here on time so that we may be at home for Thanksgiving dinner." The big engineer looked at the roll of bills and then at the men and said, "Gentlemen, this is lovely of you and I appreciate it beyond words, but I cannot take it, for, to tell you the truth, my train is just twenty-four hours late and should have been here this time yesterday."

In the Christian life we should endeavor to be on time. We should put first things first and not allow things of the world to interfere with our spiritual progress. We should be on time in giving a kind word or a word of appreciation or doing a kind deed, so that in due time we may receive the reward which is laid up for those who love and serve the Lord.

18

OLD OXCART

"For my yoke is easy and my burden is light."—MATTHEW 11:30.

IT WAS a great convention of people from all over the state. The hall was crowded to capacity. The next speaker was to be a Southern man of national reputation.

As he came to the platform, the audience rose, and, with white handkerchiefs waving, gave him a silent but impressive salute. We waited eagerly to hear what his first words would be.

His voice rang out clear. "Ladies and gentlemen, I came to your convention on the Louisville Nashville." At this point I almost forgot where I was. It seemed as if I could hear the train caller, and my mind ran to the beautiful scenery along the Louisville Nashville road, with its picturesque panorama of splendid scenery. With his next sentence, the speaker brought me back and made me think of a Chautauqua lecture. These were his words: "Forty years ago I came over this road on an old oxcart. If I should have had to come that way today I would not have been here in time for this gathering. I would say nothing against the mode of travel of our forefathers, for they it was who made possible the development of the present. Neither would I continue to ride in an old oxcart, with more modern methods of travel all around me.

"The change from the oxcart to the Louisville Nashville is not doing away with travel. It only changes the mode, and gives results more comfortably and in less time."

The Church of the living God can well afford to use the best methods to get results, without doing away with the work of our forefathers and the traveling Godward.

LOVE

"Love never faileth."—I Corinthians 13:8.

THE sale of papers was poor, leaving the little newsboy only a few pennies to spend for a birthday present for his little invalid sister.

He stopped at the florist and asked the price of the flowers, but found them too expensive and turned to go, when the clerk said, "Here, my boy, take these and plant them and you will have some beautiful flowers."

The boy was delighted and hurried home down the alley, picking up four tin cans on his way. He filled them with earth and put in the bulbs. Then he set them in the window near his sister, and while she could not understand why he gave her this kind of a gift, yet she appreciated the love that prompted it.

Days passed, and with care the bulbs began to grow. The first one grew up and fell over and she tied it up to a stick. It grew a little higher and fell over, and once more she tied it to the stick. And still it grew, and it became necessary to tie it near the top of the stick.

The next plant put out two green leaves that grew with edges like a saw. The next one grew up, with two green stems and a lovely bloom on each stem, and the stems were crossed. The other one never bloomed and was rather odd, as it put out two green blades rather broad and covered with stickers.

One day, as the sister was looking through the window and admiring the plants, she discovered that they spelled a word that meant more to her than anything else in the world—L O V E—and her eyes filled with tears of appreciation and gratitude.

Remember it is love that prompts good deeds, and may we always show our appreciation to those who love us and are trying to make our lives brighter with their deeds of service.

THE LIGHTHOUSE KEEPER

"And my God is the rock of my refuge."—Psalm 94:22.

THE lighthouse keeper climbed into his little boat and pushed off for the mainland. He had planned to be back in time to light the big lamp just before it grew dark. He soon reached the shore, and making his boat fast, hastened to the little town to make his purchases. Then he came back to his boat to return to the lighthouse.

As he neared his boat, he was stopped by two men, who said, "We must detain you. If you stay with us peaceably, we will not harm you." These men had planned to keep the lighthouse keeper away to prevent him from lighting the big lamp, so that the rest of their gang could rob the ships that were sure to lose their course in the darkness. But they had not reckoned on the service of the lighthouse keeper's little daughter, who had climbed the winding stairs many times with her father and watched him light the big lamp, and knew just how it was done. When she realized it was growing dark and the time had come to light the lamp and her father had not returned, she knew something had detained him. Taking the long taper, she climbed to the top, and with the little light lighted all the big burners, until the great light flashed out over the ocean to be seen for miles.

When the men on the shore saw the light come on, they knew that their plans had been foiled. They released the keeper of the lighthouse and he made his way back home. He commended his little daughter for her good deed. He told her how she had not only saved his life, but kept the ships from being wrecked and robbed.

The constant training of youth in the home, in the Sunday school, and in the church, for Christian service is sure to bring good results. They may be depended upon to do the right thing at the right time.

21

MONEY

"Jesus said, It is more blessed to give than to receive."—Acts 20:35.

EVERY government has its medium of exchange which we call money. On this money have been placed emblems and words to show its value. The designs are arranged so that it is difficult to counterfeit without detection.

Some coins have mottoes on them which convey the spirit of a nation in a word or sentence. United States coins have three inscriptions, "Liberty," *E Pluribus Unum* and "In God We Trust." The dime and the cent have all three.

The faith expressed in the phrase, "In God We Trust," has been a great factor in the history of America as a nation. Our leaders in the past, when in a crisis, went to God in prayer, and without that trust in Him it would not have been possible for them to have accomplished for our nation the great things they did.

However, not every one in our fair land trusts in God. Some would add the letter "L" in the word "God," just after the "O," and when this is done it reads, "In Gold We Trust." It seems some have made this their motto, leaving God out of it, and forgetting that everything which we possess belongs to God and that we are but His stewards. Some day we are to give an account of our stewardship. Will it be found that we have put our trust in God or that we have left Him out and put our trust in Gold?

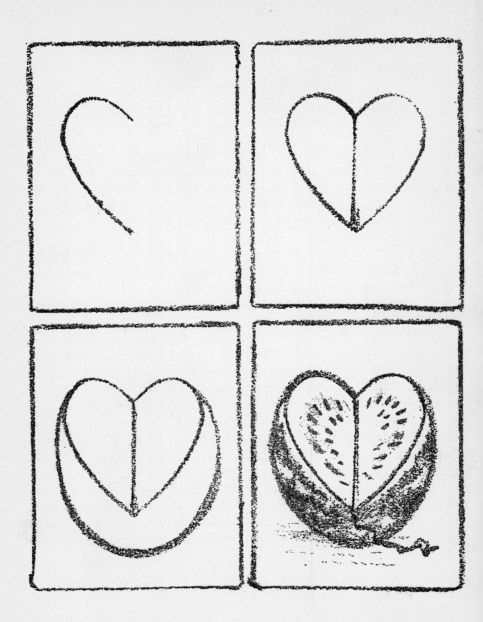

22

WATERMELON

"For with the heart man believeth unto righteousness; and with the mouth confession is made unto salvation."—ROMANS 10:10.

SOME people in this old world of ours seem to be only half-hearted, hooking into others, always complaining and acting as though they enjoyed their weakness, but not seeming to get far with it. Like a fishhook, they are dangerous to everything near them. A fishhook is good only for fishing. When it gets out of its place there is trouble.

It would be better for such people if they could be whole-hearted, filled with love for every one, so filled that every one could see at a glance their loving disposition.

If one is filled with whole-hearted love for a cause, he will begin to grow.

If the laws of nature are right, and investigation shows that they are, it is wise to use the color she uses to signify growth, that is green. Do not think that just because you are green you are growing. That would be sad indeed. However, if one is faithful in service to others he is growing and enlarging his own life.

Sometimes shadows will come thick and fast. Tests and trials, disappointment and discouragement, will almost break one's heart. But these things should not bother one if he is true, for, after all, this is the kind of a heart that we like best.

Out of one melon come hundreds of seeds, each capable of multiplying into other hundreds of seeds. So out of every good deed planted in a good heart is the possibility of reproducing many good deeds through their touching others.

23

OAKS

"For he that soweth to his flesh shall of the flesh reap corruption; but he that soweth to the Spirit shall of the Spirit reap life everlasting."—GALATIANS 6:8.

THERE was once a man who owned a large piece of ground and was very desirous of owning the adjoining land. Although a large sum of money was offered, the owner refused to sell. But he was finally persuaded to rent the land for one crop only. Papers were signed to that effect and the rent was paid in advance.

Some time later the owner noticed that men were measuring the ground and getting ready to plant something, so he walked out to ask about it. "Oh," said the men, "we are working for the man who rented this land from you for one crop and we are preparing to plant acorns at certain places in the field." "But," asked the owner, "how long will it take to grow an oak?" "Four hundred years," said the men. "In that time they will grow into big trees, and while they are growing, we will build a stone mansion between the acorns planted in the ground you would not sell, but did lease for one crop."

There are those who would not sell out to sin; would not even want to be classed with law violators or sinners, but who would not see any objection to renting out to sin for a season—for one crop.

If Satan can only get your consent for one crop, he will sow your youth with acorns of sin, which will influence you for life.

24

RESCUED

"Let your light so shine before men, that they may see your good works, and glorify your Father which is in heaven."—MATTHEW 5:16.

I SHALL never forget one story a minister told to illustrate the truth of his message.

He spoke of taking a trip across the ocean and how he enjoyed it. The thing above all else he enjoyed was to stand on the deck in the evening and watch the sun as it sank to rest amid a flood of golden hues. He said, "It seemed to me that God had taken the western sky as a canvas and was using all the colors of heaven to portray His love. It was so grand that no artist could ever paint it. One day, after looking long at the fading clouds, I returned to my room and was thinking of retiring, when I heard the cry, 'Man overboard.' My first thought was to rush to the deck and help rescue him. Then I thought I might be in the way of the sailors whose duty it is to take care of such cases. So, taking my light, I held it close to my porthole, trying to see out. It was all dark out there, and thinking my light might be some help, I held it there and prayed that the man might be saved from a watery grave, and if he was a Christian man that he might be spared to greater service in the Lord's kingdom, and if not a Christian that he might be given another opportunity to accept Christ.

"In the morning I inquired about the man who had fallen overboard. 'Oh,' said one, 'he fell over on the starboard side and so near the boat that the search lights reached out too far to see him, but, as luck would have it, a light appeared at a porthole, which helped us to rescue him.' After inquiring the number of the porthole, I found that the light which I had held was the light that had made the rescue possible."

All around us are those who are going down in the billows of sin. Are we enough concerned in their rescue to do what we can to help save them? We must let our light shine.

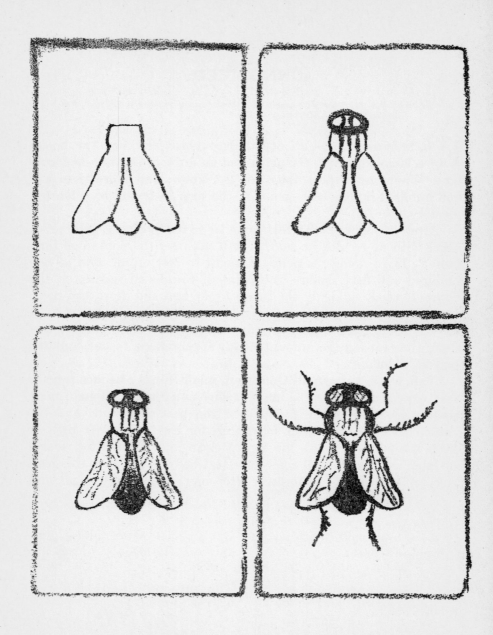

25

UNNOTICED

"Lay up for yourselves treasures in heaven, where neither moth nor rust doth corrupt."—MATTHEW 6:20.

FOR several months an expert accountant searched the books of a large company, trying to find an error of one hundred dollars. Whom to suspect they did not know, and more than the one hundred dollars was spent by the firm in trying to solve the mystery.

After the accountant had gone over the books a number of times with no results, he said, "I will run over the books one time more." In so doing his pencil chanced to rest on an item of one hundred and fifty dollars, the point of the pencil resting on the figure 1, when suddenly the figure broke and slid down the page. Examination showed the supposed figure 1 to be the leg of a fly that at some time had become pasted in front of the fifty dollar item, thus raising the amount, to all appearances, to one hundred and fifty dollars.

This was a very small thing, but small things ofttimes become very expensive. A sneer, a laugh, a slighting remark, though small, sometimes changes the attitude of the best of friends and has caused them to lose their friendship for each other. It pays to keep the pages of one's life record clean and correct, for, sooner or later, our record will come to a test before the Lord, the great Accountant, and one little sin or error may cause us to lose our soul.

26

SHORE LINES

"Launch out into the deep."—LUKE 5:4.

A SUCCESSFUL farmer, finding that the market in the little town across the water had better prices than his home town, decided to take advantage of those prices.

Gathering his produce and placing it in his boat, he rowed over to the other shore. Fastening his boat, he took out his produce and found a ready market for it. He spent the day shopping, and when night came on he made his way down to the boat. The wind had blown the boat up to the shore and he stepped in. Placing his packages in the boat, he picked up the oars and began to row. Thinking of the success of the day, he forgot everything else. He rowed for hours and finally said, "What! can I be lost in the sight of home?"

He put a hand in the water to see if he could tell which way the water was flowing. He turned his boat the other way and rowed for hours more. Finally, after rowing all night, he found, when dawn came, that he had failed to unhook his boat.

There are those who wish to go somewhere, but do not cut the shore lines. They are tied to some habit or way which hinders them from accomplishing their desire. Let's be sure to cut all shore lines for the Master's service and launch out into the deep of his boundless love, finding service for Him a great blessing.

27

PICKING CHERRIES

"The eternal God is thy refuge, and underneath are the everlasting arms."—DEUTERONOMY 33:27.

TWO brothers were picking cherries from a well-loaded tree. After they had picked all they could reach from the ground, the older said to the younger, "Here, George, come, I will make it possible for you to reach some cherries which I can not reach." So holding the little fellow upon his shoulders, he carried him where the cherries could be easily picked, and it was not long until their pail was full of the luscious fruit. This could be accomplished only by their working together.

In every community there are boys and girls who may need help, a boost toward better things. Some need help toward an education, some toward the Christian life, others in making decisions for life. There are others who need help along special lines of education that will enable them to take responsible positions and successfully carry on to become leaders among men, able to give greater service to mankind. While it may not be possible for us to attain all that we would like to have or to be in this life, yet we may be able by the little help or boost we can give another to put him in a better position than that which we have had and thus make the world a better place in which to live.

"If we do our best,
God will do the rest."

28

PROCRASTINATION

"To-day if you will hear his voice, harden not your heart."—PSALM 95: 7, 8.

A LARGE vessel, named *Central America,* while sailing the high seas, sprang a leak and began to sink.

She hoisted a signal of distress and waited for help to come.

Another ship saw the signal and came close. The captain, taking his trumpet, called out, "What is wrong?" The answer came back from the sinking ship, "We are badly damaged and are going down. Stand by until morning, please." "Let us take your passengers on board now," said the captain of the rescue ship. "Stand by until morning," came again through the trumpet of the sinking ship.

About two hours later, the lights on the sinking ship were missing. Although no sound was heard, the ship and all on board had gone down to the fathomless deep. When morning came, there was no sign of ship, crew, or passengers.

There are thousands of people today sailing on life's sea toward an unknown port. They are on the ship *Procrastination,* and although they realize that delay means danger, they, too, think there is time enough yet.

They hear the call of our pilot Jesus asking them to leave all, to follow Him and come aboard the old Gospel ship *Zion,* where there is safety and comfort, and which at last will bring them to a sure anchorage in the eternal haven of rest. They hear, but delay.

Life is so uncertain that one cannot afford to put off his day of salvation. There is danger and death in delay.

29

THE COMPASS PLANT

"I am the way, the truth, and the life."—JOHN 14:6.

MANY interesting things can be found on our western prairies, the different grasses, sage brush, bird and animal life, that are quite different from other sections.

One large plant, known as the compass plant, is especially interesting. This plant grows from three to ten feet tall, and has large yellow flowers, which measure from two to four inches in diameter.

These flowers have very short stems and grow quite close to the main stalk. Its name was given the plant because of its leaves, which always point north and south. Trappers, hunters, Indians, and travelers, who knew of this, could tell the direction even at night.

This fact has been denied by some, but a careful observer has proven that the young leaves, standing edgewise to the earth, always point north and south. The older leaves often become covered with dew and dust, and the extra weight causes them to lose their power to stand erect, and they may be found pointing almost in any direction. This plant would be of no value to the traveler who came to it for guidance if it were not for the newer leaves, which are free from dust.

How much like the compass plant every Christian should be. As the compass plant points to the north, so the Christian should point to Jesus Christ under all conditions, keeping free from the dust of sin, which would cause him to lose his influence for good and point untrue to those who might look to him for help and guidance.

30

SIN

"Likewise reckon ye also yourselves to be dead indeed unto sin, but alive unto God through Jesus Christ our Lord."—ROMANS 6:11.

TWO boys who were very dear friends, and attended the same school, decided to sit together.

One of the boys, Frank, lived on a farm and brought apples to school. The other boy, Bill, lived in town, and his father operated a general store, so he brought candy and the boys exchanged with each other and became quite chummy.

One day Bill said to Frank, "Come, let's have a smoke. I will furnish the tobacco." But Frank, having been taught that smoking was a bad habit and injurious to one's system, refused. Another time Bill asked Frank to drink. But Frank's parents also had taught him the evil of drink, so again he refused.

A few weeks later the same boy asked his chum to come with him over the hill to play cards. He said a big gang were playing over there and they would teach him how to play. Bill insisted. But Frank said he knew his father would not want him to play cards and he did not care to learn to play.

Time passed, the boys grew to manhood. One day, after Bill had taken a smoke and several drinks, he picked up his deck of cards and made his way down to an old box car to have a game of cards with the gang. While the game was on, a dispute arose over the cards and the men quarreled. A fight followed, and Bill took out his revolver and killed a man. Today he is a murderer and serving a life term in prison.

Frank became a Christian and later a minister of the Gospel. Today he is a great blessing in the community in which he serves. When relating his experience to me, Frank said, "Had it not been for the influence of Christian parents and the Godly example set by my father, I might have been the convict today instead of a minister of the Gospel."

31

THE PRODIGAL

"I will arise and go to my father, and will say unto him, Father, I have sinned against heaven, and before thee."—LUKE 15:18.

THE story of the Prodigal Son asking for his portion of his father's estate that he might go out in the world and spend it as he pleased, has been repeated many times in life.

This young man, after receiving his portion, left his father's house and care, and went into a far country to have what he considered a good time.

Soon all he had was spent and he began to be in want. Then his thoughts turned homeward to father and plenty. He thought that if his father would only take him back he would offer to be one of the hired servants. He knew he was not worthy to occupy the place of a son and felt very humble; but his father saw him coming when quite a distance away, and ran to meet him. There was a reconciliation, and instead of becoming a hired servant as the boy requested, he was reinstated in the home once more, a feast was held in his honor, he was given a new robe, and a ring was placed on his finger.

It would be difficult to imagine any father doing more for a wayward son than did this father on the return of the Prodigal.

Suppose that when this young man was leaving the far country to return to his father, he had decided to bring with him some of the things he had found there and had returned with a pig under one arm and a bundle of husks under the other, it certainly would have been most disgusting.

When a child of God who has wandered away in the paths of sin decides to return to his heavenly Father, asking His forgiveness, he must leave the things of the world behind and make a full surrender of himself to God. Then he is reinstated into God's family, and becomes a member of His kingdom and an heir to His love.

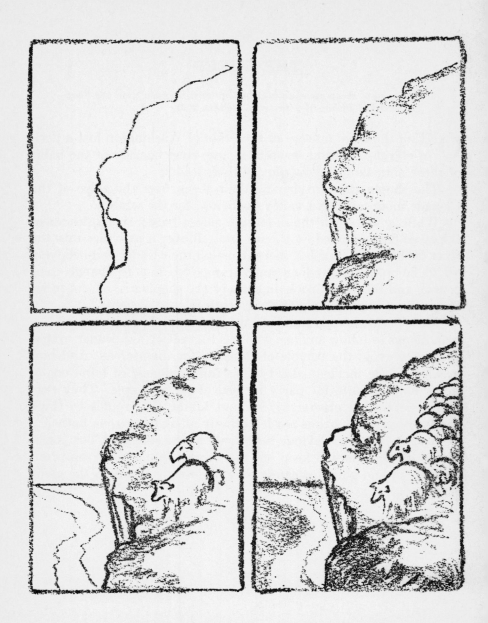

32

THE SHEEP

"For ye were sheep going astray; but are now returned unto the Shepherd and Bishop of your souls."—PETER 2:25.

ONE of the large ranches of the State of Washington lost a flock of eleven thousand sheep in a large river because of the habit of these animals to follow blindly their leader.

The shepherds were driving their sheep over the slope of the Cascade mountains to a valley far below, for the winter.

While going down the mountain side a trusty sheep, leader of the large flock, slipped on the ice and fell over a precipice into the river far below. The other sheep, trusting their leader and believing all to be well, followed on until it was too late to change their course, and the whole flock, in spite of the shepherds' efforts to restrain them, went blindly to their death.

How perfectly this parallels the tendency of thousands of human beings to follow any one who sets himself up as a leader so that they may avoid the trouble of thinking for themselves. And how accurately the incident also typifies the proneness of hundreds of individuals to vote for party instead of for principle. They read and believe what others say, without taking the trouble to think for themselves, and thus are led blindly along dangerous paths.

Jesus Christ our Saviour is not only a true shepherd, but is also a true leader. He will keep our feet from slipping over the precipice of sin and guide us safely over the rough places to the green pastures.

33

THE WORM

"Be sure your sin will find you out."—Numbers 32:23.

THE beautiful rose with its lovely fragrance, its long stem covered with thorns, was growing in the garden. As I looked at it, it seemed to have a message for me in its perfection, every velvet petal in place as though a fairy had arranged it so, with the dew of the morning clinging to it like jewels.

I plucked the rose for a sick friend, and, to my surprise, the leaves and petals began to fall off, and it was but a moment before I was holding in my hand just the thorn-covered stem, all that was left of a once beautiful rose.

On examining the stem carefully at the top, I discovered the reason for my surprise. A small worm had quietly worked its way into the center of the rose weakening the petals and causing them to drop off at the first disturbance.

How much like the little worm is sin, which creeps into the heart, unnoticed and unsolicited, doing its harm by leaving character spoiled and reputation ruined.

The act that causes confidence and faith to fail may be small, but it is deadly.

Sin is very deceiving. All sin comes short of the glory of God. "Be sure your sin will find you out."

"Come unto me, all ye that labor and are heavy laden, and I will give you rest."

Character is what you are. Reputation is what folks say about you.

34

FAITHFUL IN SERVICE

"Moreover it is required in stewards, that a man be found faithful."—
I CORINTHIANS 4:2.

A N INTERURBAN train makes the round trip from Franklin to
Oil City, Pennsylvania, a distance of sixteen miles, taking on
and letting of passengers at Reno and Monarch Park.

It does this each hour of the day, every day of the week.

It would seem to get monotonous, the same thing over each day,
the same trip between the two cities and back again from where it
started.

It would become monotonous, no doubt, if that were all. But
the trip is not all. The motorman is making it possible for people
to reach home or office and is helping them on their way to do their
daily tasks.

There may seem to be monotony in our religious work. Sabbath
services, scripture, songs, preaching, prayer, and Sunday school last
week, this week, and next week—last year, this year, and next year!
We seem to be just where we were last year. But what of the year's
trip?

If, in our round of duties daily, weekly, yearly, we are able to
help those in need to their proper destination, something worth
while has been done.

The service rendered is not in vain if humanity has been helped
Godward. That is what Christians live for, to help men to their
proper destination. Be willing to go the round of duty, and you will
learn that your life is not narrow and useless, as you may have
feared.

35

JEALOUSY

"Thou shalt not covet."—EXODUS 20:17.

TWO men lived on adjoining farms. Both farms were of good fertile soil and well located. The houses stood on the slopes of the hills facing each other. Hedges were planted around the edge of each farm to give an artistic setting.

When one planned anything new for the home or farm, the other would do the same. When one would build, the other would duplicate it, no matter what it might be.

One day the house at the left of the road was painted red, and the very next day the house on the right became its reflection.

One farmer planted flower beds, and the other did the same. One made a new roadway around the hill, and a few days later another was winding around the hill across the road.

It seemed that the pleasure these two farmers might have had was sacrificed to a spirit of competition with each other. As a result, they became angry with each other and were enemies.

It reminds one of two chickens pecking at an ear of corn. Each one is determined to have it. A few grains are picked off by each chicken. Then their greed increases, their feathers begin to rise, and a fight ensues. The corn is forgotten.

It is not difficult to understand why chickens or animals act thus, but is it not surprising that human beings made in the image of God and destined for eternity should be envious of each other and act in such manner?

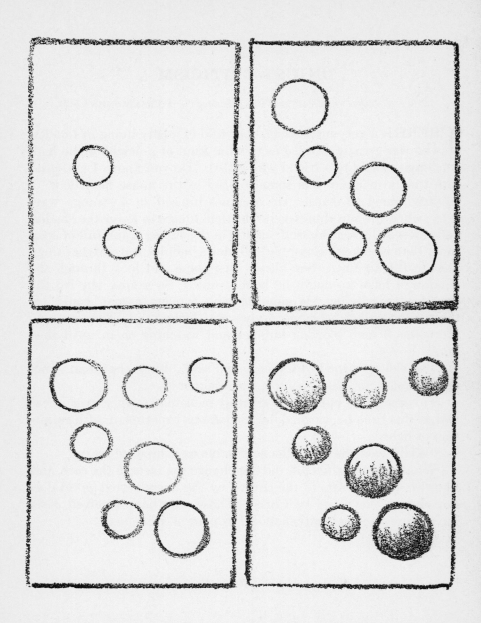

36

UNJUST CRITICISM

"Prove all things; hold fast that which is good."— I Thessalonians 5:21.

THERE is a very interesting story told of a lady living in London who was greatly puzzled as to what kind of a neighbor she had. One day she said to a friend who called, "Do you know, I am quite sure that a madman has come to stay in the house next door. I am frightened to death. He occupies himself in a strange way. Why, when the sun shines so bright that I have to lower the shades, you can see him seat himself outside in the sun by a tub full of soap suds; then he takes a clay pipe and blows bubbles and watches them float in the air until they burst. Just come and look through the window, I have no doubt he is at it now." So saying, she led the way to the window. Wondering who the crazy man could be, the visitor pulled back the drapes and looked out. Sure enough, there was a man blowing bubbles and watching them until they burst.

The visitor turned to the lady and said, "Why, that man is not crazy, that is Sir Isaac Newton, the scientist."

This man was one of the greatest men that science ever knew, and at this time he was making his famous experiment with refraction of light.

"Well," said the lady, "he acts to me as if he were crazy."

What the lady thought, did not change the facts in the case, and, likewise, the criticism of the church by the unconverted world does not change the power of Christ. Those who have received Jesus have proved to their satisfaction His plan of atonement.

37

OUR FEATHERED FRIENDS

"Behold the fowls of the air: for they sow not, neither do they reap, nor gather into barns; yet your heavenly Father feedeth them."— MATTHEW 6:26.

THOSE who have made a study of birds tell us that these little feathered friends are a great blessing to humanity. If it were not for the birds the human race could not long endure. Destroy them, and in a comparatively few years the insects will have multiplied to such an extent that trees will be shorn of their foliage, plants cease to thrive, and crops fail to grow.

Many birds prefer to live near homes; they soon learn who are their friends and where they are welcome. Every bird has its own way of speaking. We may understand their calls if we pay close attention and try to remember.

What birds have you seen near your home? Have you seen or heard the robin red breast? Listen to his call, "Quick, quick, do you think?—What do you, do you think?—what you do, do you think?"

The crow does his best to sing, but can only say, "Caw-caw."

The cedar bird says, "Tze, tze, tze." The quail says, "Bob White, Bob, Bob White—more, more wet." The bluebird seems to say, "Purity, purity, I—oh, purity—dear, dear, think of it, think of it, I, oh, purity."

The calls and songs of many other birds are very interesting. They teach us the lesson of praise to our heavenly Father. Like them, we should praise our Maker and remember that if we carry out His plans in our lives we will prove a blessing to others.

38

MISSIONS

"Redeeming the time."—Ephesians 5:6.

IN A beautiful mansion on a large tract of land near the ocean
lived a wealthy gentleman.

At one place the land extended out into the water, making an
ideal place in which to view the passing ships, and the owner had
his gardener plant a palm tree there. Later on, when the tree was
large enough to lend shade, the owner had his workmen place a seat
under its wide-spreading branches.

One day, as he sat there enjoying the ocean breeze, he saw a
sailboat going by close to the shore, and was so impressed with it
that he decided that was just what he would buy, so that his family might enjoy trips on the water. Next, a large ocean steamer
came in sight, and as the man watched it he said, "That is one of
those missionary boats taking missionaries, I suppose, to some far-
off country. What nonsense! They say they love their folks, yet
they leave them to go off to some foreign port to wear their lives
away preaching to the heathen. I do not believe in it. The sailboat for me."

While he sat musing, he fell asleep. He seemed to be in a strange
country, sitting at a window opening out on the ocean. It seemed
he was one of those who had never heard of Jesus and was sitting
looking across the waters, wondering when the missionaries were
coming to tell him of the Christ. He was glad to awake and find
it was only a dream and that there was yet time for him to help
answer the longing of the heathen for spiritual light.

BOY OVERBOARD

"Who can understand his errors? Cleanse thou me from secret faults."—
PSALM 19:12.

A SHIP surgeon told the story of one of his experiences.

"On one of our trips a boy fell overboard. The crew was ordered to save the boy. One of the men pulled him up on deck. They removed his outer garments and applied methods of resuscitation. When they had done all they knew how to do, they said, 'Have we done all we can?' 'Yes,' I said, 'I think you have.' Then a sudden impulse caused me to see what I could do. Bending over the boy I found it was my own son. You may well believe I did not think the last thing had been done. I took off my coat, bent over him, blew into his nostrils, and breathed into his mouth, I turned him over and begged God to bring him back. I worked for four long hours, and just at sunset I began to notice the least flutter of breath that told me he lived. I learned my lesson. I shall never see another boy drown without taking off my coat and from the very first doing all I can to save him."

O that we would work just as hard trying to save other boys and girls from a life of sin as we do in trying to save our own.

The test comes to the true Christian to do his very best at all times. God is no respecter of persons. Christ died for all, and we should do our best to save others from the paths of sin, getting our minds off self and fixed on Jesus.

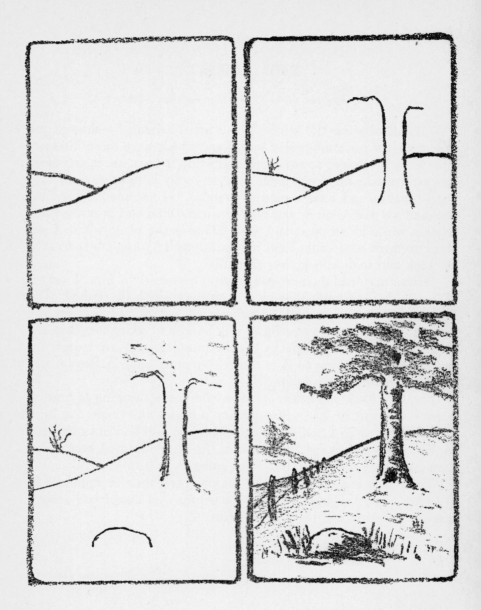

40

THE ARTIST

"I must work the works of him that sent me."—JOHN 9:4.

WHILE visiting the studio of an artist friend, he showed me many of his studies and paintings, which were most interesting. Then he looked at the clock and said, "I have an engagement this afternoon, and if you wish, you may stay here or go with me; but I must go as I have a picture to paint." I accepted the invitation and we were soon on our way down the lane and over the hills. After a while he stopped and said, "This is the place where I am going to work, and while I get my paints ready you go over to that old rock and take a look over the hill."

It was a splendid view and when I returned to him, I asked, "Why do you not paint that view from the rock?" He replied, "Oh, I came out here one rainy morning, placed my canvas on the ground, and with an umbrella in one hand and paint brush in the other, I painted that view in twenty minutes, and my reason for calling your attention to it is that the picture sold in Boston last week for one hundred dollars."

I walked back and again looked at the scene thinking of how on a rainy morning he had spent twenty minutes and made one hundred dollars, while I had spent the afternoon and had not made my car fare. I remembered that back in the studio he had said, "You may go or you may stay, but I am going."

The lesson is a good one. We may use our time or squander it. We may allow things to interfere or we may go ahead and accomplish that which will be of most value.

41

SHARING THE LOAD

"We are laborers together with God."—I CORINTHIANS 3:9.

EVERY Sunday school should have a cradle roll, a home department, and junior, primary, and intermediate departments, each with its superintendent and teachers. Much can be said in favor of each of these departments; they are important and we must have them.

One Sabbath, while going out to visit a little country Sunday school, I overtook a man and asked him how his school was getting along. "Oh, it's a fine school," he said. "What makes it so fine?" I asked. "Well, sir," he said, "we have a good superintendent; he is always there, no matter what the weather. Rain or sunshine, we can count on him. We know he will be right there and go ahead with everything."

I visited the school. The superintendent rang the bell, passed the song books, led the music, and would have played the organ if he could. He led in prayer, taught the adult class, passed out the papers, and conducted the closing exercises. After the prayer, he asked my name and I told him, and he said, "Oh, you are the missionary. If you had told me, I would have had you speak." I replied, "If you had asked me, I would have told you."

No superintendent should try to carry all the load. The work should be so divided that all may feel they have a part in helping to make the school a success.

Sometimes we treat God as these people treated their superintendent. We have such implicit faith in His ability that we think He will carry on the work without us. But it is quite a mistaken idea. We are laborers together with God, and He expects each one to do his part, however small or great that part may be in building up His kingdom here on earth. True, He is our burden bearer, but the work is ours and He giveth strength for our day.

42

SAILING

"Let us hold fast the profession of our faith without wavering; for he is faithful that promised."—HEBREWS 10:23.

IT WAS early morning, with a good stiff breeze blowing up stream. Flakey clouds floated by, while the sunlight played on the waters of the river, giving reflection to the foliage which fringed its edge.

Two men were standing on the shore gazing at the little village on the opposite side. "I would like to go over to that little village," said one of the men. "Well," said the other, "I have a friend who has a boat, he will take us over."

Calling to his friend, he arranged with him to take them across. The friend came down the path, carrying with him a long pole with canvas roped around it. He laid this in the boat, and told the two men to climb in. "But where are our oars?" asked one of the men. "Come on, you need not worry, I'll get you over there. This is a sail, we will sail over." "But," said the other, "I do not understand. Look, the wind is blowing up stream and we want to go across the stream."

"Just step in the boat and we will show you." So the men stepped into the boat. The boatman set the sail, which caught the contrary breeze and began to pull the boat through the water. With a rope fastened to the sail the man guided the boat across the stream. After making their purchases the two returned to the boat, and by turning his sail at a different angle, the man who was doing the sailing caught the same breeze that took them over and made it bring them back again.

In life there are times when the ill winds of adversity may be harnessed to prove a great blessing for service.

43

A VISION

"Come unto me, all ye that labor and are heavy laden, and I will give you rest."—MATTHEW 11:28.

A MINISTER was asked to assist a missionary in a meeting which was to be held among the hills in the southern part of one of our middle states. After the missionary had met him at the train and assisted him to his home with the baggage, he suggested they go for a walk around the town.

It was a warm afternoon, and the places of interest were some distance apart, but the missionary suggested they go a little farther and get a wonderful view from the hills. "But," said the minister, "suppose we go there another time, I am getting a little tired." But the missionary insisted that it was only a short distance, and they walked on. As they made a turn, there was a hill right before them, with a winding path up and over the top. The minister thought there would be no pleasure in climbing that hill and was just ready to refuse to go farther, when he noticed there was a tunnel through the hill. The tunnel was dark and dirty, but, oh, the beautiful bright sunshine as they stepped out at the other end and the glorious view they had of the landscape in all its beauty. It was well worth the extra steps to have seen it.

Many times in life when the way seems long and hard to travel, and one grows a little weary and is almost ready to give up, it really pays to trust and take a few steps farther, for at the end there await us new beauties in Christ Jesus, and we will feel that it has paid to go all the way.

44

SANDY

"A new heart also will I give you, and a new spirit will I put within you."—Ezekiel 36:26.

A COLLEGE professor being in poor health was advised by his physician to take a complete rest.

He decided to visit an uncle who lived twenty miles from a railroad station in a quiet little home nestled at the foot of the Tennessee mountains, with a trout stream gurgling by.

Here the weary man could read, fish, sleep, dream, rest, and enjoy life as he wished. He soon became acquainted with Sandy, a red-headed, freckle-faced boy who passed that way carrying the mail. He was always whistling and happy.

After missing the boy for a few days, the professor visited him and found him too ill to be taken to the hospital. The professor came each day to see the boy, and read the Bible to him. One day the boy asked to keep the book until the professor came again.

One morning a message came, "Sandy wants to see you. Come quick." When the professor reached his bedside, Sandy said, "Oh, I am glad you came. Professor, do you think I am a Christian?"

The professor said, "Sandy, if you believe you are a Christian, I believe you are." Sandy looked up and said, "I believe I am a Christian." His arms dropped to the bed and Sandy had gone to meet his Maker. The professor realized as never before that God has a purpose in our plans. He had been instrumental in bringing life eternal to Sandy.

45

CONQUERING DIFFICULTIES

"But where sin abounded, grace did much more abound."—ROMANS 5:20.

WHILE yet a small lad, it was a real pleasure to go with my older brothers to the field where they were doing the spring plowing.

I remember there was a large rock which lay in the center of one of the fields, covered with briers and weeds. When the plows started, father would say, "Be careful, boys, there is a large rock in that clump of briers." At last he decided it was time to try to get rid of it. He placed a crowbar under the edge of the big rock, and with another rock placed under the crowbar, began to pry. To his surprise, the stone began to lift and break. On examination, he found that it was soft limestone, about four inches thick. He then took a sledge, and with a few strokes broke it in pieces. The boys came in the wagon and hauled the pieces away, the briers were cut, and the ground plowed and corn planted.

For years this stone had defied the plows. It had conquered because it was feared. But when father determined it must go and set to work on it, it was conquered and had to go.

There are times when we allow difficulties to conquer us, and because of fear we do not make the progress we should. The sooner we attack our difficulties by an organized plan or a strong blow of perseverance, the more easily we may conquer them.

46

LINING UP THE LIGHTS

*"Then spake Jesus again, saying, I am the light of the world: he that followeth me shall not walk in darkness, but shall have the light of life."—*JOHN 8:12.

STANDING on the wharf, I looked out over the wide stretch of water as the great lake seemed to push away from me in every direction.

It was evening, and as I stood there enjoying the beauty of the scene and talking to a friend, the lights of the harbor began to appear.

"What are all these lights for?" I asked. "Oh, those three lights you see at the end of the harbor?" said my friend. "The one far out, the one close in, and the one on the ship points the way for the ship to a safe landing in the harbor. Those three lights must line up as one light to give the pilot the exact position of the landing."

Jesus said, "I am the light of the world," and Jesus, God, and the Holy Spirit are one and will direct our lives into the great harbor of His love, where we shall be protected from the storms of life.

When one is desirous of knowing God's will, there are three things which always concur: first, inward impulse; second, the Word of God; and, third, the trend of circumstances:

God is the heart impelling you forward in the right;

God, in His book, the Bible, corroborates whatever He says in the heart;

God in circumstances which are always indicative of His will.

47

THE VIOLET'S CONSOLATION

"Be strong and of good courage."—JOSHUA 1:9.

IN THE springtime, when the flowers begin to push their heads above the ground, and long before some of the wild flowers have even thought of making their appearance, you may see the little violet making its bow on the hillside and in the woodland.

One day, while the little violets were pushing their purple heads above the dead grasses and leaves, they heard a voice.

The large oak tree was looking down on them and seemed to say, "Ho, you little violets, you may just as well be content to stay where you are. You can never grow strong and tall like me. You can never amount to anything of value. Why start? Look at me, I am strong. I have faced the storms of many a long winter. In the summer I lend my shade to many a weary traveler, and when I am through here, I will be cut down, perhaps, and shaped into a mast for a large ship that will carry great cargoes, and I will rule the winds at will. But you, so small, so frail, so weak, you cannot do anything or ever amount to anything."

One little violet looked up admiringly and said, "O great oak, you have stood the storms of many a winter like a giant. Your spreading limbs lend shade to many a weary traveler who comes your way. You may become the mast of a ship and serve humanity, but, great oak, the same God that created you, created me, and I, too, may be a blessing. Perchance there may come some one this way picking flowers, and I may be taken into a sick room to bring blessing and cheer to some discouraged heart."

Every one may be a blessing where he is, if only he is willing to be of service to others. God created us and has a plan for each of our lives. Little things are of as much value as the big things in God's service if they fit in His plan.

48

THE QUESTION MARK

"It is good neither to eat flesh, nor to drink wine, nor anything whereby thy brother stumbleth, or is offended, or is made weak."—ROMANS 14:21.

A LITTLE fellow began to ask questions of his uncle. After a few of them had been answered, other questions began to come so fast that there was time only for an occasional answer with a yes or no. Time was kept on the little fellow, and it showed that he asked forty-two questions in two minutes.

It might be asked here, "What will be the answer to this question mark?" You can see that it turns itself into a boy, and it has been said that every boy is a question mark, for it is a question what he will turn out to be. He sees some one put a cigar or cigarette up to his mouth, and although he is mistaken, he thinks it looks manly and says, "Well, if he can do that, why can't I?" So he puts one in his mouth and begins to smoke.

Later, he sees some one put a glass of liquor to his lips and drink its poisoned contents, and he again makes a decision and says, "If he can do that, I can do the same," and he starts with his first glass. It is only a short while until this same boy, who has always been well respected by his friends and has been the pride and joy of his parents and family, has step by step disgraced the whole family and made a hog of himself.

You may laugh at this picture, but when the finished product is seen on the street, it is no laughing matter.

Here is a problem and the youth of today are going to have to help solve it.

They have within their hands the molding of the character of the coming generation. It is a stupendous task, and the question is, Will they be able to cope with it?

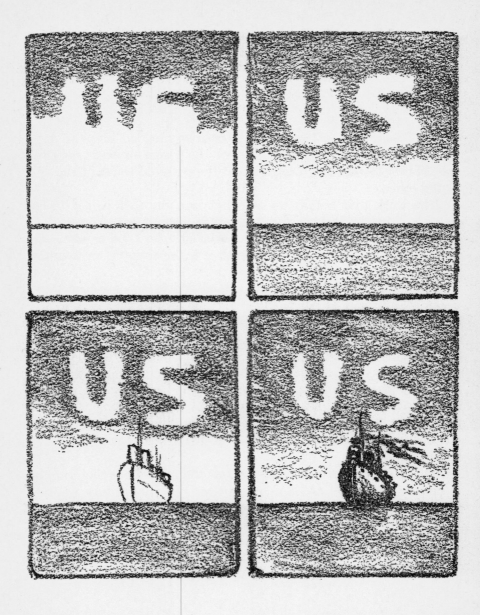

49

US

"And hath made of one blood all nations of men for to dwell on all the face of the earth."—ACTS 17:26.

THE background of America has been so blended into the government that some have failed of the vision of their own responsibility toward the foreigner and the personal touch of the one to the other.

The work that befalls us is to put into the picture the background of brotherly love, for America is what it is because of us.

There is no country in all the world quite so good as our own. Naturally, the country in which we live is the country we love the most.

Those who have left their homeland and loved ones across the ocean seek a land of peace and plenty, a land of liberty, and the right to worship according to the dictates of their conscience. Some have come with their virtues, but many have come with their vices, and it seems quite evident that if we do not make Christians of the latter, they will make heathens of us.

It is not enough to teach them the Constitution of our government and the principles for which it stands, but along with this should go the spirit of true American citizenship, which is Christian citizenship that always stands for the highest and noblest things in life.

The enforcement of law is good, but the love of obeying the law is better. Therefore, to be a good citizen one should love to obey the law as well as see to it that our laws are just.

50

CROSSROADS

"Jesus saith unto him, I am the way, the truth, and the life."—JOHN 14:6.

WE HAVE all traveled along many different roads. There are roads that are broad and smooth, others that are narrow and occasionally rough. We must often travel the narrow and rough roads when they lead to our destination, for though the driving may be more pleasant on the broad and smooth highway, if it is not headed right we will never reach our goal.

I would rather be headed right than be a mile on the road going the wrong direction. I know for I have had the experience.

We hitched up old Dobbin and drove along the road up the hill. Coming to a little white house with green shutters, we asked the way to Sheep-run. "Oh," the little lady said, "you have made a mistake, you should have taken the road to your right at the crossroads. You are just a mile out of your way."

We had to return to the crossroads, take the road to the right, and start over again. But having done this, we were soon at the end of our journey.

So in life, as we travel its highways and find we have made a mistake when we come to the crossroads, that we have taken the road to the left, which leads to sin and destruction, instead of the road to the right, which leads to eternal peace and blessedness, let us stop and inquire the way back and return to the right road, with a determination to keep on that road until we have reached our destination, our heavenly Home.